SKY SANDWICHES

JOHN F. BUCKLEY

ANAPHORA LITERARY PRESS

COCHRAN, GEORGIA

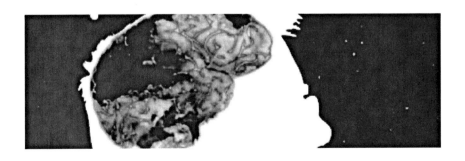

ANAPHORA LITERARY PRESS
163 Lucas Rd., #I-2
Cochran, GA 31014
www.anaphoraliterary.com

Book design by Anna Faktorovich, Ph.D.

Cover Image Designed by: Raquel Buckley.

Proofread by: Todd Glass.

Published in 2012 by Anaphora Literary Press

Sky Sandwiches
John F. Buckley—1st edition.

ISBN-13: 978-1-937536-32-9
ISBN-10: 1-937536-32-7

Library of Congress Control Number: 2012945999

SKY SANDWICHES

JOHN F. BUCKLEY

PRAISE FOR *SKY SANDWICHES*

I love John F. Buckley's work. His humor, energy, and charisma burst out of his poetry. I love poetry which comes to life, is personified, and hits on his girlfriend. I love when his youth comes off the page, and I get to relive a Michigan childhood. I love the way every narrator falls into a doomed love with every woman he meets. I love his heroic immigrants. And I love the humanity that all of his characters have and the humanity that is clearly the center of this talented poet's being.

— John Brantingham, author of *East of Los Angeles*

John F. Buckley's *Sky Sandwiches* is a five-course Michelin meal. Buckley is a well-traveled Bukowski. He has a way of peeling back the pain in a lost relationship. It makes you want to look away but you can't, just like passing an accident on the highway; you're scanning for glass and blood. This collection cradles the reality of modern popular culture that is imbedded in our psyche. Buckley raises his glass and invites you in the den. The chairs are worn but comfortable, just like at Grandma's in the basement when the TV was turned on. He is a master at revealing the scars one line at a time. He explores diners in Michigan, final yard sales and crushed Californian dreams. Buckley doesn't lock his doors and has his weathered foldout chair perched right on the rim. He is to be savored as his words caress the sadness that comes from the pain of living. This is one meal you don't want to miss. Straighten your hair, snap that napkin on your lap, and prepare to deliciously dig in. *Bon appetit.*

— T. Anders Carson, author of *Death Is Not the Worst Thing*

In his first solo full-length book of poetry, *Sky Sandwiches*, John F. Buckley serves up an engaging concoction of humility, self-deprecating humor, classical references, the sensuous pleasure of well-placed words, and a keen observation of humanity's tenderness and limitations. From the plaintive opening line of "Saturday, 10:30 AM," *I need you so badly right now* to the bleary-eyed awareness in "The Morning After" that *the sun lives in a plastic bucket down in St. Croix, not here,* the only thing better than eating sky sandwiches at home is hearing Mr. Buckley deliver them at the podium. Buckley's *sui generis* facility with language at once conveys personal angst and sweeping universals. A must-read.
    —Marta Chausée, author of *Resort to Murder*

Surrealism is one of the most ruthlessly understood concepts in art, a veritable coat rack upon which artists have hung every excuse for provocation. In *Sky Sandwiches* by John F. Buckley, the poet reminds us that surrealism is not an end but a means. His incredible imagery, wordplay, and humor all combine to summon a world at once real, urgent, and familiar.
    —Brendan Constantine, author of *Calamity Joe*

John F. Buckley has mastered the art of absurdity. Trilling a surrealist high note while striking the bar chords of narrative, *Sky Sandwiches* proves that eccentric imagery and galumphing streams of diction enhance emotion and create empirical phrases of melodic motion. "Eco-Poem" and "Portrait of a Dying Marriage as an Unplugged Refrigerator" are just a few zany classics in this paradise of poetry.
    —Cory De Silva, editor for Bank-Heavy Press

Reading John F. Buckley's poems is like romping through a modern-day painting by Hieronymous Bosch. In Buckley's world of "deadpan pansies" and children "seedy as zucchini," poems are likely to have lives of their own, in some cases even spending hours with "cruel but effective speech therapists." The poems in *Sky Sandwiches* travel the landscape from menace to whimsy, stopping along the way to tickle the imagination at every turn, yielding a lively and entertaining read throughout.

    —Tamara Madison, author of *Wild Domestic*

John F. Buckley's *Sky Sandwiches* is made of meaty, heart-stopping, delicious poems—not the flavorless variety that leaves you unsatisfied, but piled high with only the finest ingredients. Hold it in your hands and indulge: this book has real nutritional value.

    —Clint Margrave, author of *The Early Death of Men*

Real, honest, and painfully humorous, *Sky Sandwiches* deftly questions the absurdity of living as a perpetual outsider in a superficial world where everyone and everything else fits. Buckley grapples seriously with childhood demons and hard-won adult truths. A language puppeteer, he effortlessly masters satire and pathos that catapult us into the "catawampus" of all we love to hate about America and its "controlling but benevolent" attitude. Here, McMansions, disappointed family members, Walmarts, malt liquor, Blondie, convents, shit tonsils, classrooms, ex-porn stars, mean fertility specialists, and hot sauce melt into an addictive and irresistible Kool-Aid that leaves us panting for more.

    — Alexandra Mattraw, author of *Projections*

John F. Buckley's *Sky Sandwiches* leaves me full-stomached but wanting more. Not just because the holy glory of food is delicately plated in many of his poems, but also because feasting on the sharp words of a poet who is unafraid to delve into what seems to be a heaping fountain of his otherworldly knowledge is a feast I wouldn't dare skip a bite of. To state it more simply, John's poems are like bread, and my brain is not on the Atkins diet.

    —Karie McNeley, author of *Sugar Rushed*, editor for Bank-Heavy Press

Strikingly real, comically tragic! John F. Buckley brings back imagination to mundane adult life by spiking the punch with everything from college poem parties to imaginary stepfathers and lots and lots of frothy food! The guy's a poetic chef digging in the kitchen to add every flavor to the entrée. It's every ounce of life on a cuisine journey that is sure to make you hungry for the filthingly beautiful.

    —Zack Nelson-Lopiccolo, author of *Dancing with Scissors*, editor for Bank-Heavy Press

John F. Buckley is that deliciously talented sous chef of poetry who now invites you to the opening of his cool joint: *Sky Sandwiches*. On the menu is a multicultural fusion of everyday life intermixed with the myths of heaven and earth, and spiced with the political and personal throughout. Here you'll see emperors seated alongside renters, evil Boy Scout masters sharing cocktails with poems masquerading as famous people, and robot pigeons and moon rabbits darting under the tablecloths. The dinner conversation is peppered with Swedish, Swahili, Polish and Mandarin accents and satisfying morsels of people striving to make ends meet, to make love work, and to make the world a place they can call home. Take a seat and let the banquet begin.

    —Martin Ott, author of *Captive* and *Poets' Guide to America*

In *Sky Sandwiches*, John F. Buckley informs the reader, "Poetry and grocery bills live in two separate worlds." And in his first collection of poetry, Buckley presents a multitude of worlds that brilliantly paint and frame the day-to-day. His poems are grounded in toughness and tenderness, in fantasy and authenticity. They are poems that offer new life, yet linger like old souls. After reading *Sky Sandwiches*, the reader will agree, "Today is when everything changes within these lines."
— Daniel Romo, author of *Romancing Gravity* and *When Kerosene's Involved*

The poems in this book have been crafted by an astute cartographer. These mapped objects together form a deceptively delicate terrain over which we may choose to wander; but be warned that if we stay long enough, only body armor and a helmet could block out the deep rumblings just below the surface of this harsh landscape. A dense and mature book.
— Paul Suntup, author of *Sunset at the Temple of Olives*

John F. Buckley's poetry shows both imagination and craft. You never know where his poems are taking you (robotic pigeons which produce kimchi?), yet you always feel secure in his hands, certain he knows where he's going, and that he will get you there safely.
— G. Murray Thomas, author of *My Kidney Just Arrived*

John F. Buckley's work urges us to step out of our world and into his. When we do so we realize it's not much different from ours; he just points out the tiny details we tend to miss, the most important ones. Through an uncanny imagination, John F. Buckley shows us what we already know but may have forgotten — the moments that make life so beautiful.
— Michael Torres, author of *The Beautiful Distraction*

for Martin and for Raquel,
for very different but very important reasons

CONTENTS

ACKNOWLEDGEMENTS

The following poems, sometimes in different forms, have appeared in or been accepted by the journals and venues listed below:

"Aching for a Knack for Charcuterie" first appeared in *Atlanta Review* Volume 18, Number 2 (Spring/Summer 2012).

"Anybody Can Live on the Moon" has been accepted for publication in *Oxford Magazine*.

"The Appointment" first appeared in *Watershed* Volume 33 (Fall 2009).

"An Area Bounded by Three Surface Streets" has been accepted for publication in the *Clackamas Literary Review*.

"At the Reunion" first appeared in *Big River Poetry Review* (June 30, 2012).

"The Authority Figure" first appeared in *The Mochila Review* Volume 13 (2011).

"Documented Immigrant" first appeared in *Poetry New Zealand* Number 43 (September 2011).

"Documented Immigrant" appeared in *Southern Humanities Review* Volume 46, Number 1 (Winter 2012).

"Domestic Ops" first appeared in *Red Lion Square* Episode 17 (October 5, 2010).

"Domestic Ops" appeared in *Ragazine* Volume 7, Number 2 (March-April 2011).

"Eating Out" first appeared in *Chronogram* (October 2011).

"Envy" first appeared in *New Mirage Journal* (Summer 2011).

"Hometown Expatriate" first appeared in *CounterPunch* (June 22, 2012).

"Island Living" first appeared in *The Midwest Quarterly* Volume LI, Number 4 (Summer 2010).

"Keep the Home Fires Burning" first appeared in *Concho River Review* Volume 25, Number 2 (Fall 2011).

"Leaving New Eden" first appeared in *Obsessed With Pipework*

[UK] Number 56 (Autumn 2011).

"Legacy" first appeared in *CounterPunch* (June 22, 2012).

"Lost Scent, Strange Mountains" has been accepted for publication in *Harpur Palate*.

"A Man and a Woman and a Bird" first appeared in Moon Tide Press's Poet of the Month feature (May 2012).

"Message to an Imaginary Stepfather" first appeared in *Pear Noir!* Number 4 (Summer 2010).

"Ode to Barabbas" first appeared in *Saranac Review*. Issue 7 (2011).

"Poem for Christy's Daughter" first appeared in *Journal of Truth and Consequence* (Fall 2009) and was nominated for the 2009 Pushcart Prize.

"Progress" first appeared in Moon Tide Press's Poet of the Month feature (May 2012).

"Protagonist" first appeared in *CounterPunch* (June 22, 2012).

"Respite" has been accepted for publication in *Other Poetry* [UK].

"Saturday, 10:30 AM" has been accepted for publication in the *Cimarron Review*.

"Short Stack" first appeared in *Husbands and Malfeasant Dogs* (December 2011/January 2012).

"Storefront Church" first appeared in *Oyez Review* Volume 37 (Spring 2010).

"Storefront Church" has been accepted for publication in *Pacific Review*.

"The Story Behind My Next Tattoo" first appeared in *The New Orphic Review* [CAN] Volume 14, Number 2 (Fall 2011).

"The Story Behind My Next Tattoo" appeared in *Obsessed With Pipework* [UK] Number 56 (Autumn 2011).

"Syzygy" first appeared in *The Mochila Review* Volume 13 (2011).

"Your Fault" first appeared in *The Mochila Review* Volume 13 (2011).

THE AUTHORITY FIGURE

Opening scene. Four in the morning. A car honks
in spastic Morse code outside an apartment complex
on the east side of South Oxfield. She, who was up
already after biting her tongue in her sleep, waking
herself with a jolt, deciding to go on patrol, finds
the sedan, forcibly pops the hood and cuts a wire.
No more noise. The driver is pissed but knows he
has gotten off easy. "Get off your ass, Jesse, and
knock on the door. Better yet, save it for morning."
Someone inside the faux-stucco building will buy
her a beer as a thank-you when they next see her
playing darts at Rico's and hard-to-get otherwise.
In the darkness, the pretty youngish sheriff adjusts
the bikini top under her khaki shirt, better securing
her .38-caliber bosom in its polka-dot holster, and
goes to her pickup where a thermos of coffee awaits.

Natalie Ampatuan Davenport, bottle-blonde Filipina,
ex-porn starlet and sheriff, now observes video chastity,
no soppy nonsense, just untelevised rural law and order.
Three years of criminology classes, her tuition paid
with money made in San Fernando Valley McMansions.
She supports solar and wind power out on the range
and sometimes officiates at pancake breakfasts and
heated Bingo tournaments over at Good Shepherd
Methodist Church. She once solved that murder among
the scruffy paleontologists working the land by the hills,
tracked down and caught the black-bonnet sisters who
held up the First Community Bank, and secretly helps
to heal emotional casualties on the high-school football
defensive line. The mayor publicly announced before
last year's Memorial Day parade, "Rusty Rock County
appreciates you," proving that life can have second acts.

I write her new life, allude to her old one by the big city,
and wonder – why? – about *Trout Mask Replica*. I recorded
it onto cassette once, off a badly scratched library LP.
I move her around like a Barbie doll, sometimes for
reasons as scattered or occluded as a Captain Beefheart
melody, but hope that she doesn't resent me for doing so,
hope that she's happy with a job in local law enforcement,
that none of the county board of supervisors will ever
run into her movies on cable. Is this an American attitude,
controlling but generous, benevolent? I've never been
there to find out. Instead, I loll and sigh around farmyards,
stuck with my great-aunt and her darkening moles in
West Pomeranian Voivodeship, drowning in *w*'s, vodka,
and poorly made *paczki*. Book me, take me in, good-hearted,
competent, pert Sheriff Natalie, save me, take me away.
I can't even speak Polish, which raises so many problems.

PROGRESS

When I was a little boy, all poems rhymed.
Not anymore. As I grew older,
poems spent many hours with
a battery of cruel but effective speech therapists.

Nowadays, poems are more neurotic,
because of the prolonged psychological abuse,
but they can do almost anything. Some poems
are doctors or lawyers. Some poems
have become firefighters or police officers. Some poems
don't like money very much, so they have
entered the field of teaching. Bruce Kardashian is
a dyslexic poem who won an Olympic gold medal in 1976.

I saw a duck who was a poem buying
crystal meth in downtown Irvine, but he
drove away before I could get his autograph.

The only time I have had any trouble with a poem
was in college at a loud party. I went there with my
        girlfriend
and this poem wouldn't stop hitting on her.
I got mad and started making fun of his accent.
I changed the ends of his lines to disgusting words
like *shit-tonsil* and *Romneylicious*. We ended up
wrestling in the mud on the lawn until the police came.
I was fined two hundred dollars, but the poem
walked away scot-free because his father was a prominent
        ghazal.
Fucking diplomatic immunity.

Despite this, I support poems' rights to vote, to marry,
and to attend good schools, even with the white children.
Outer space, poems' rights, and the ocean depths
are the three final frontiers.

ENVY

I read his lines and I trace his carvings,
how he slices the language and stacks
different unpredictable, perfect
pieces together,
stanza after stanza, theme after theme,
varied yet unified,
and I thrash my legs in frustration on the sofa,
letting my thigh muscles tremble
like fat on a lily-white brisket.

Maybe if I met him,
I'd act like the smirking tattooed guy
selling tri-tip on soft rolls today
off a gas grill outside Albertson's,
who called me *sir* five times in three sentences,
who meant *asshole*, as if
he thought I thought
I were better than him
for having lean arms, wearing glasses,
and not working on a hot Sunday.

It was pretty good tri-tip, but
I could make better sandwiches than either of them,
toasting the bread,
slathering the condiments evenly
from one side of the crust to the other,
calculating the ideal proportion of
meat to cheese to vegetables,
spearing an olive on a toothpick through the top.
And I can write cleverer poems than one of them.
Because I care. Because I compare.

Somewhere between a butcher and a surgeon,
somewhere between Dagwood Bumstead and the man
who eats one circle of bologna on white bread,
there I am,
a journeyman verbal deli worker,
still a bit green
but seasoning into a pastrami swami,
Sri Beefysattva, if I have my way,
if nobody else gets a vote.

A PROMISE

This story doesn't end well for any of them.

There were,
and I really can't stress this enough,
not these days, three children, all,
as the saying goes, as seedy as zucchini,
three rather unwholesome children
just on the cusp of learning
to do such things as rolling bomber joints,
drinking schnapps competitively,
writing huge black whorls of cursive graffiti,
and necklacing ideological opponents.

I didn't know them anymore by then; I was going to
what was assumed to be a better school,
a safer school, by that time.
But before, when I knew them,
the congenitally furled nail on my left pinkie toe
had been ripped away, I forget how, and
a small piece of broomstraw or raw spaghetti
became embedded in the pink jelly
underneath where the toenail had been,
causing my toe to become infected,
causing me to have to wear my slippers to school,
to walk to the bus stop several blocks away
while wearing soft, red plaid, bedroom slippers.

This was before I discovered
my interpretation of "appropriate social behavior"
did not perfectly align with other people's.

This was before the vast gelatinous mass
washed up on the beach of Sylvan Lake,
wiping other matters from the minds of
the neighborhood people.

This was long before the humming violet night
of nineteen-year-olds in Windsor, Ontario.

No, at this time, an awkward boy with a purulent toe
limped to the bus stop and found those three children
          waiting
with fistfuls of rocks, with sturdy, stamping boots, with thin
          smiles.

As I said, this story doesn't end well for any of them.

The first boy becomes bloody and broken,
afraid to become the protagonist in his own novel for many
          years.
The reader is, so far, left unfulfilled, disappointed.
And those three children, long since grown and moved
          away,
pursuing careers in law enforcement or ethnobotany,
will inevitably meet horrible deaths,
scrupulously agonizing deaths,
if I have anything to say,
if I have to sit here writing until the end of time.

GENEALOGY

The grandmother has anticipated my arrival,
wrinkling a forehead dotted with skin tags and
tilting a magenta-crayon lipsticked mouth so that
I must kiss the spider-legged mole in the corner.

Suckle upon her long wisdom, she implores me,
of perfecting stuffed cabbage, crocheting winter hats,
and spreading a history of self-regard like fertilizer
over the lives of grown children potted like lilies.

I see my mother's desperation pinned like a black
ripe grape between the molars of her mother's pink
dentures, make the ward against hexes, and recite
Philip Larkin's verse to a Perry Como melody.

"Come here, honeychild. Grandma needs the moon.
Only you are tall enough," tugging me by the earring
she says she has seen only dirty Negro men wear,
frowning at the beard unsuited to an ex-altar boy.

The moon is a candy-store convent, a proposed sweet
second home for success, a poppy-seed kifles poised
just beyond reach, just enough fine powdered sugar
sprinkling down from the sky to speckle my forehead.

I spend my time stretching, the third generation, now
bereft of ancestral sorcery, Yankeefied thoroughly but
wishing for Magyar nightscapes, the lights in the sky
a beacon instead of a reminder to crane, arch, and twist.

AT THE REUNION

Charcoal grills speak the lingo of early-millenium
hotbox confessionals throughout July afternoons,
each chef uncle a whispering penitent inventing sins.

A tidy lather of yellowjackets, slick bodies same
as soap flakes, drown drunk in the clear juices
of burger patties cooling on serving platters.

The line between callous honesty and cruel
chicanery has been drawn in hot mustard on
a half-charred bratwurst, tearing eyes either way.

Four greedy children, five pieces of fried chicken.

You found me drawing a ketchup mandala there
on the tablecloth, fakeblood focuser of third eyes
smeared by clumsy stray palms, sinking my heart

through the loss of enlightenment's crimson path,
that last phrase like a battle hymn title, the name
of a thrumming ode to some wet flesh harvest.

Grandma's got the camera again; somebody takes
it away before she misfires and crops people's
heads off, initially capturing their souls but then
letting them waft out through severed necks.

Sissy has a sunburn, rubbing angry pink shoulders
with cold buttered cobs, stray grains of salt
scraping welting tracks across her papery skin.

Open containers of potato salad and coleslaw
arrive from the supermarket deli, transparent
crucibles of mayonnaise and unseen factors.

Watermelon babies man tables with cold green smiles.
The catawampus surging of their keenness squirts
awry like warm, black seeds pinched inexpertly
between fingers and thumbs, typically striking
some objects or persons next to their true targets.

Everybody's drinking the watery red Kool-aid.

By the end, I can't comprehend. Images fall through
my fingers like ice cubes slipping onto a freshly
mown lawn on the way to a glass, stray grass
and dirtflecks soiling the task of interpretation.

DOMESTIC OPS

On another swollen summer night,
stricken by the shadows of agents
strumming sullen adagio banjos
on the street outside our avocado
split-level ranch, she sets traps
for the maturing apocalypse. I must
study Mandarin and speed chess
down at the local community center,
tonal syllables and ivory gambits.
His job is to roll out a nylon mat
five times per day and comb the dog
for bugs and fingerprints. Our sister
learns to dazzle with sinuous displays
of flaming nunchaku and cymbals.
All of us have to hunt for and gather
nutritious wild plants from vacant
residential lots in the neighborhood.
We ask her why again, leery of specters.
She opens the back of the record player,
spinning the turntable at 78 rpm
with a bloody-cuticled index finger.
Out pops four dull sapphire capsules,
one for each secret molar compartment.

MESSAGE TO AN IMAGINARY STEPFATHER

If you informed me the world was a gumball
dyed blue, the flavor of contact-lens solution,
that clouds were sublime lint,
that the whole sticky orb lay forgotten in the dark
pocket of a ten-year-old Shiva's Tuffskins, awaiting divine
     molars,
then I would believe you,
because you've almost never lied to me,
only about the important things,
which are broad enough and significant enough
to hold complex relationships with the truth.

You could tell me bedtime stories of
Anubis the evil scoutmaster,
who forces Webelos from Thebes to hunt snipe
among the dunes of the Sahara
until long after their last flashlight has burned out,
leaving the troop to the darkness
and the hungry shades of jackals.
I would snuggle beneath my comforter and drift asleep,
free from nightmares of divine judgment, deceit, and
     predation,
knowing you stayed vigilant,
no farther away than one of several local bars.

If you enlisted in the Marines
but gave them my name instead,
so that they came pounding for me with their carbines and
     khaki,
sneering, "Let's go, maggot. Time to man up,"
I would forgive you, even as I learned I'd apparently
volunteered to dismantle IEDs for the next twenty-four,
thirty-six, oh, no more than forty-eight months,
for it's true that I need to get in shape and learn discipline.
My best interests and the country's best interests
are often aligned.

You have pulled stunts,
like when you were caught sprinkling curly hairs
into the crème brûlée I'd struggled to master all day.
(Yet maybe what you added was shaved vanilla bean,
improving the dish and my status as a chef.)
And after we shot our amateur porno,
bringing us closer together (I felt),
you excised your face from all footage,
labeled the only copy *Rendezvous with Gherkins*,
and sent it out for festival consideration;
that upset me for a bit.

But after everything real and potential that we've been
     through,
after the filthy camping and whispers,
the inside jokes and shame,
what continues to bother me most
is that you won't adopt me.
I've paid the county fees and filled out all paperwork.
Each night, its folder slides beneath
the door of what I call your study.
All you have ever had to do is sign once.
I will do all the rest.
Still, each morning shows
an empty space above the bottom line.

SEVEN COURSES, NO ISSUES

You can host a fancy dinner party for less than twenty dollars, provided your home already contains certain ingredients. You can host a fancy dinner party that no one will ever forget, that will be commemorated on your tombstone, murky legends of which the future dominant species will speak of in their cathedrals, awed by the zenith reached by their primate predecessors.

For an appetizer, pick something light. Go to the mechanic downstairs, that sturdy woman with the iron-gray mullet, and ask to borrow some lug nuts. Fill their holes with pimento cheese. Wrap them in bacon and deep-fry them for twenty or thirty minutes. Tell your guests not to chew; you don't need extra dental bills. Have them simply overcome their gag reflexes and swallow the porky-cheesy-metallic nuggets in their entirety. Get ready to perform the Heimlich on those who simply refuse to follow directions.

Remember the chilly, blustery, winter days of childhood? Remember what Mother used to make you for lunch on those gray afternoons? Ice cubes and chilled cat food, which is why you ripped up her living will and left her hooked up to the respirator for those long years after the accident. Didn't you want soup? Don't you love your dinner guests more than your parents loved you? Give them soup. Mix three packets of soy sauce from Panda Palace, half a gallon of contact-lens solution, a large can of Veg-All, and several handfuls of Swedish meatballs from the frozen-food section of Costco. It's easy!

Nobody likes salad but everyone appreciates the effects of sufficient roughage. Skip the lettuce and such in favor of enemas. Gather everyone in the living room, break out the portable massage table, the aquarium tubing, the gallon Baggies filled with leftover soup, and grow closer as a community.

The fourth course, the palate cleanser, should be a piquant formic-acid sorbet, saturated with little black specks that aren't bits of Tahitian vanilla, but ants, ants from the counter, ants from the wall, ants from behind the kitchen cabinet, ants from inside the living-room ceiling. Just as Native American tribes like the Lakota Sioux were surrounded by bison, and thus ate bison aplenty, so are you surrounded by ants. You've scrubbed everything and kept the sink free from dishes, but the ants thunder across all surfaces, coursing everywhere but into your personal orifices and throughout your body. Until now.

Some go for poultry as a fifth course, but chicken can be expensive. Heat pasta, either instant ramen or Spaghetti-Os. Keep the noodles simmering in a big pot of water on the rear burner of your stove for what? Three hours? Is that long enough? You shouldn't have thrown out the directions. You should have made a test batch. Now they will know, they will know and judge and leave you just like Daddy. They will scamper out the door, smoking their pipes and smelling like cheap whiskey, neglecting to give you a goodbye kiss, jauntily jangling their car keys, looking away as you sob in your flannel footsie pajamas. On the flip side, there will be more overcooked starch paste for you.

The main course calls for a *tour de force*, an entire elk roasted on a spit in the living-room firepit. Make sure to start cooking the skinned, gutted carcass by the end of the third course, or it may not be finished in time. Other than that, don't think; do. Let the momentum of the meal carry you forward.

Dessert is a cake baked in the shape of an aluminum bathtub chair, a subtle reminder of our shared aging and mortality, the prevalence of household accidents, the end of the meal, the mounting apocalypse. Not everyone needs a piece. Robots need no cake. Robots don't eat. Also, you need no cake. I need hardly explain why.

IRON CHEF

It's been decades since the litterbug
whom you and I saw sow the street
with white fast-food wrappers was
loudly called a pig by you through
the open window of the blue Pinto,
the first car I remember our family buying.

Now you spend money on surplus
kitchen implements and masses of food
for the two freezers downstairs, reasons
to cook at home and avoid restaurants,
or at least avoid standing in line with
your thick, purpled, thrombotic legs.

Now you prepare the remaining years
like thawed venison neck roasts braised
in accordance with a schedule for when
guests are visiting, perhaps eventually hungry,
especially a Very Special Guest who will
someday ask you to leave with Him.
Has the litterbug already answered such a request?

Freed from youth and ex-wives, your
intermittent explosiveness toward your
fellow man has quieted in the meantime,
aside from whatever propels you to strew
right-wing emails throughout my inbox
and very occasionally interrupt dinner
with hot barks about intellectual arrogance,

making us children reel and the peas cool
in their serving dish, leading me to cry,
ridiculously. You never cry, due to some
better masculine spirit, the kind forged
in steel-jacketed wartime generations
long ago before the hippies apparently
spoiled everything with welfare fraud and
wrappers wet with Coca-Cola and secret sauce.

Try to ignore the liberal bias of the teardrop.
Try to ignore how it wastes fortitude, trading it
for sterile sentimentality, as your firstborn son does,
creating whining poems instead of grandchildren
in the solemn autumn of your life,
swapping pens for productive hard-ons.

As he makes his mistakes, watch silently,
perhaps resigned at litanies of loved ones'
bad decisions but respecting any exercise
of divinely-granted free will, American choices.
"You with the ears," that's all you'll say,
"What do you think you'll want for dinner?"

ACHING FOR A KNACK FOR CHARCUTERIE

The freezer is full of Lean Cuisine. White cartons
of leftovers moisten and wither in the food hospice

of the fridge. Today, the weather is cloudy and cool.
I ache for a knack for charcuterie. I fantasize sides of

beef and Boston butts, grinding them into homemade
kielbasa, the links of kings, grilled Polish sausage and

good mustard filling the monarch's gut before battle.
It was all laid out in a magazine, a hot red food-porn

money shot, reminding me of making them years
ago with my aging dad, so much handier than I,

his electronic meat grinder and multiple yards of
natural casing, one of us feeding the chopper, one

creating happy endings at the spurting nozzle,
each swollen arc tied off with a knot of white twine.

Nothing was weird that afternoon, nothing paused
unduly or awkwardly, just two men wrangling meat,

socking some goodness away for winter, and maybe
some, three apiece, set aside for that night's dinner.

THE MORNING AFTER

Almost well before noon, the first one awake.

The sun lives in a red plastic bucket down
in St. Croix, not here. Rising like an otherwise
graceful white egret crippled by plantar fasciitis
from the army cot in the spare bedroom. Into
the broken antelope carcass of the living room
to traipse delicately amidst the unlikely foliage
of last night's rash drunken family gathering
and this week's insufficient local newspapers.

On the dinner table, open albums of photos
of grinning toddlers in plaid wool lederhosen,
of megatherium-hunting parties from the 1970s,
back when grandpas drank Wild Irish Rose
and spat warm Skoal juice into Pringles cans.

Ibuprofen my father, cold coffee my mother.
A heart like a runny egg. Lungs like twin loaves
of garlic bread riddled with Parmesan abrasions.
There they go, *pump-a-dump*, a bit slower each day.
(No more cigarettes, no sloped pipe affectations.)

Shit, shower and shave: one way to cure zombies.
No more brains, no more shambling, no more
panting after the quick, after the established fact.
Life seeps again in the shadowy hollows of man.

THE APPOINTMENT

Obedient, wanting to please the fertility specialist,
I dip my scrotum into the beaker of boiling water and
leave it to steep for three minutes. I add cream after,
to thicken the infusion, anything that will help.
But holding the specimen up to the light, the doctor
frowns, proclaims, "This is not yet tea," pours the
contents into the sink, and reads the pubic hairs
arranged like wet leaves at the bottom of the glass.

He will not tell me what he sees, instead asking,
"Are you a virgin? Have you ever suffered a grievous
injury to your pride? Did the basement walls of your
childhood home contain imprudent levels of rayon?
How many high-voltage power lines run through
your bedroom? Is your microwave fully insulated?
When was the last time you tasted pungent cheese?
What sort of man are you, in honesty,
what sort of man?"

I clumsily confess to him our private affairs,
how after we make love, I take my wife out to
the fertile green courtyard, pick her up by her ankles
and swing her around, how the mini-plunger works
to extract my last milky drops, how we devoutly pray
to household saints Dr. Seuss and Mother Goose,
burning dried Gerber's strained peas like incense
at our living-room shrine. He nods and passes
back behind the heavy curtains, leaving me waiting,
aging, my Saharan loins aching.

He comes back into the room with an unlabeled tin
and a newsletter. "In this box is a dark, rich type of
lapsang souchong. It will resolve your difficulties but
cost you your firstborn child. Brew it in your tears.
This is the newest copy of *The Pennysaver*.
Check the section on yard-sale adoptions; some couples
have made lucky finds." I thank him and tell him I'll
sleep on it, walking out to the waiting room, to my wife,
my entire family. "Baby, I'm ready. Baby, let's go."

PROTAGONIST

Though my marriage is mighty, my closet
is filled with honeymoon suits that no longer fit me.

I will instead assume the mantle of hero,
wearing it like a poncho of heavy yet eminently breathable
    fabric,
sewing bright purple fringes down its sides
so that when I raise my arms in warning,
dastards in black hats can more clearly see their doom
    approach.

But first I will clean off the grime of ages
with several trips through the washing machine
(warm, gentle cycle),
bolstered by Woolite and OxiClean,
reinvigorating the mantle for a new epoch of heroism.

I will fluoridate the Pacific as my inaugural feat,
no kidding around.

I will reinvent dinosaurs,
then slowly braise them for days
so that the world may not run out of fossil fuels.

I will reach the belly of the whale and tickle it,
freeing the wayward prophets and sodden Pinocchii.

I will learn to distill tequila from concentrated agape,
a drink that obviates thousands of armed conflicts
and tens of millions of broken relationships.

Better ways of apportioning limited resources
will shoot in blue beams from my fingertips.

Such is the power of the mantle of hero.

My wife will adore me again.
Many will adore me, but as I will get by
on only fourteen hours of sleep a night,
there will be no time for autographs.

Yes, many saw my creation of the medical-marijuana
fruit loop as a mistake, perhaps even a tragic one.
And yes, mistakes were made.

Still, weigh my deeds in the balance,
except for the interlude with the tennis pro;
all good teachers drop the lowest grade,
and the same logic should apply here.

SYZYGY

Lonely astronomer, eyeing the pills and bourbon,
    whispering
Give me codependence or give me death, wished upon a star,
met a thin woman who smoked through a tortoiseshell
    holder,
something she had ordered from a developing-nation's
    airline's *SkyMall*.

Five years and fifty pounds apiece later, no more cigarettes,
lunches of portion-controlled salmon and salads, they both
    have learned
through trial and error to ask invisible main-belt asteroids
    for favors.

Twisting through the void of space, 18956 Jessicarnold keeps
    each load of laundry
snuggably soft and wrinkle-free, though they must still do
    the folding themselves.

5822 Masakichi lets the leftover take-out chicken rest in the
    fridge
two extra days without going rancid, while 66458
    Romaplanetario
made a relative success of their first attempt at homemade
    walnut pesto.

22348 Schmeidler extends the working life of his disposable
    razors,
leaving his face stubble-free and thus kissable for that much
    longer.
(He wonders why it took so long to learn that she didn't like
    his beard.)

And thanks to a word aimed at 2133 Franceswright, the long
        line
at Best Buy last month, when she was late getting back to
        work,
suddenly moved quickly.

They don't have sex that much anymore, not since both
        exclaiming
oh god,14605 Hyeyeonchoi, thank you within split seconds of
        each other.

Once he prayed to 934 Thüringia as he spent an office hour
        sliding
guilty eyes down the cleavage of one of his students, but
        when
she looked up, smiled at him, and said he was her favorite
        professor,
he remembered it was actually a minor planet: *too much
        power, too much force.*

Now he sticks to petitioning tiny 9478 Caldeyro for pleasant
        dreams
before his Sunday-afternoon masturbation and nap sessions;
she doesn't like those, feels almost cheated on, asks 24699
        Schwekendiek
for some brief impotence and a little more attention.

Wish after wish flits upwards past the exosphere,
shifting orbital paths and probabilities, subtly shaping all of
        the small worlds
they craft for themselves, marbles with pilots, airless,
        magnetic and reeling,
past perihelion, into aphelion, together apart.

YOUR FAULT

It's your fault that the stars go out at night
and whore around, making their mothers
cry into teeny-tiny teacups brimming with
alkaline tears and heavy cream, bitter brews
saved for when wayward children come
home, climb back up the stairs to the skies,
pull up the covers, and claim to make only
innocent constellations – the racecar bed,
the dustpan and broom, the china-face dolly.
But the cigarette smoke in their nighties
smells like you, the gasoline on their pajamas
is you, the sugarfree sweetener sprinkled
all over the window sash, the rolled dollar
bills and bent spoons are you, you, and you.

It's your fault you did not read bedtime tales
of global warming and financial collapse, of
horror yawning over the coasts and crests,
didn't sow enough warnings to make dreams
of solutions to get us all out of these messes,
those turds on the floor of the boardinghouse
pantry. Don't make a joke, pantomiming
you'll fry them like sausages; they're always
just stinky links, signs of your oversights, sins
and crabapple subliteracy, sour aversion to
research and fairy-tale data. Now look at them,
nestled in quilts with their tranquil pink faces.
No agon, no sparagmos, no social anagnorisis
will come in their nightmares to save us all.

It's your fault you loved me for loving the love
that you showered upon me in springtime,
the season of updated prescriptions for Abilify
and recreational Haldol, regardless of chronic,
irreparable personal shortfalls, my psychic
resistance to everything vital. You purchased
me irises like a resolute pupil orphaned on
Father's Day, hoping that Teacher would give
extra lashes and kisses and lessons, as if it would
ice all the bruises you suffered while plucking
flowers from burly old pensioners' gardens
while his own heart melted, its atria riddled
with crystal-clear rivulets, thawing trickles
from ventricles eroding a road to the ocean.

These are your faults and many more, more
than enough to send you down grumbling to
South Yardtown for processing, send you
downhill with bags of cement to fill the mixer,
the trough and the facial molds. But you slid
and retired inside me – again! – slipping
inside till the spectacled hounds went away
to the next house. So here you squat, tucked
in my noggin, poking your thumbs through
my nostrils and wiggling them shamelessly.
You must cease and desist, or I'll give you up,
tattletale fountains of evidence leading them
back here to seize you and take you away
from me, one last desertion, one last crime.

A MAN AND A WOMAN AND A BIRD

Thirty days have passed
since buying the robotic pigeon
I hoped would bring us closer together.

You had sighed admiringly at
the lifelike model from Japan,
rife with real synthetic feathers
and able to conduct aerial tea ceremonies.
We could not afford it,
so I bought a slick South Korean version
with painted slate-blue plumage.

It cannot fly, I understand your
disappointment over this,
but nevertheless, it bobs
its head, coos, has an internal
atomic alarm clock,
and ferments in its abdomen
certain types of kimchi in half the time.
If a person ever wanted certain types of kimchi
in two weeks instead of four weeks,
this was unquestionably the model to get.

I forgot you don't like kimchi.

Having been the one to lose the receipt,
I am more than willing to help you pack,
I am more than happy to wish you luck
as you search for a man who can offer you
more than second-rate birds and breadcrumbs.

If you stay, nothing will change.
We will continue to take
our South Korean robotic pigeon to bed with us,
propping it between our pillows,
an avian chaperon,
allowing it to peck us awake
in the morning at the proper time,
waiting for its battery to fail,
for its springs to lose elasticity,
for our warranty to expire.

PORTRAIT OF A DYING MARRIAGE AS AN UNPLUGGED REFRIGERATOR

Sitting on top, gathering dust, are a copper
head-tickler and an overpriced basket, both
from the faux-quaint yuppie swap meet
held each Saturday two neighborhoods over,
storing your rejection letters.
(I meant (not really)
your not-quite-yet-acceptance letters.

Up in the freezer, next to half-finished
orange popsicles lying on a torn wrapper,
is one tiny bite left of what used to be
a commemorative slice of wedding cake.
And all you can say is you were hungry
and I wasn't home when I'd said I'd be.

Down in the crisper are the golden apples
of consequence, the heavy fruits of matter,
which have been lolling there since before
we knew how to remember. The blackening
and softening meant something to us, but
we tried hard to stay naked and unashamed.

The meat drawer is empty, except for some
ketchup and some honey-mustard dip for
long-since-devoured McNuggets. The drawer
has fallen off the tracks, onto the bottom,
and someone has a foot in it, toes bursting
an unknown packet. What is that sour smell?

Locked inside the main compartment are we,
two kindergarteners who kidnapped each other,
clinging to and pinching each other for comfort
and vengeance, t-shirts soaked with chilly sweat
and breath condensation, twin ransom notes
held to the front of the locked, handleless door

with cheery-colored magnetic plastic letters.
I won't add more as it's a foregone conclusion:
bloody socks on the rim of the tub each month,
passive-aggressive love notes, forks of rankling,
and deep dreams of spleen. Everything at all
in these past nine years invariably leads to now.

SATURDAY, 10:30 AM

I need you so badly right now.

I need you to come over and help me
secretly make fun of the things at this yard sale.

When I had that near-death experience
last year and went to Purgatory for a while,
this is the kind of yard sale I saw
all over the place over there. This
is the kind of yard sale designed for
the not quite good enough for Heaven
and the not quite bad enough for Hell
and the not quite restless enough to become ghosts.

This box contains nothing but
a single, spring-green, nylon ankle sock and
a vintage, faintly radioactive, highly flammable
pair of small boy's pajamas. They turn
bright red in the presence of urine and
bright blue in the presence of blood,
a confusing nightmare for both
the accident-prone bedwetter and his parents.

Over here is a set of four Spanish-language
personal-enrichment cassettes
unlocking the secrets of *Muchos Ganadores*.
I don't know them.

This cat is not for sale, but the people here
say he should be, for having diarrhea in the garage
soon after they used the rest of the litter
to soak up the oil stain beneath the Accord.

I actually like this framed chalk drawing
of an adobe church in a vineyard,
forever at rest amidst the hum of bees.

Everyone eyes but nobody touches
the used hand-molded ashtrays,
the clothespin Christmas ornaments,
the sticky-looking lanyards. They hold
children's love juju that doesn't belong to us.

Look in this box of paperbacks.
Somebody really likes bad science fiction.
These people on this front cover look like us
before we gave up, back when we thought
we would make it. But the artist failed to capture
my overbite. You used to cherish my overbite.

You said if I ever fossilized in your presence,
you would remove my underdeveloped lower jaw
and hide it from the archeologists.

That was back in the house in Fresno,
long before our last yard sale.

1953
for Paul Suntup

I don't think you remember properly.

It has been fifty-nine years since
I became every "Like" button on Facebook fan pages.
I had been trying to impress a girl I was dating.

She was impressed only slightly
but she still called it "unduly" impressed.
She just didn't get it.
How could she?
Then she broke up with me and married
another man, a swineherd with a lisp.
She had babies. She had hideous
translucent rat babies with Rottweiler jaws.

The United States at the time of my
transformation needed such heroism as mine.
Nothing good was on television yet,
while the Soviet Union was making
petrifying progress in the field of socialist vaudeville.
Mandarin oranges were oppressing the citrus workers of
        China,
and we just knew that things were going to blow over there.
Valor was going for thirty dollars an ounce – not
the cheap whipped petrochemical stuff in tubs,
but the good stuff, the frothy essence of valorous beans.

All of this is where I came in. All of this
is when I turned into a rallying cry for
every special thing you've ever
commemorated since childhood.
The convertible sofa-toaster ovens.
The rye-crisp surfboards.
The girl in the Paul Suntup poem
with tigers at the ends of her fingers.
The tragic blue sky with the hollow clouds,
billowing and puffy like valor. Or meringue.
The comfort of an uncle's touch on Thanksgiving.

Positive reactions radiate from me
like orange lines around a first-grader's
drawing of a sun, like nuclear noodles.

Is it so much to ask for a rocket ship,
that I may go forth and seek love once more?

LEAVING NEW EDEN

Edna, oh god, Edna, and Phyllis, why
did you let your garden see me like this?
After my love-bout with a fistful of
dirt-flecked radicchio fresh from its bed,
I must take the walk of shame
past the turgid tomatoes and zucchini,
past the long rows of tall corn
to the rural highway taxi stand.
Damn it, spring greens are feisty,
but they won't leave you cab fare.
In the distance, the tittering pussy willows
mention my full name and address,
including my middle one and apartment number.
Did I leave my wallet? I think I left my wallet.
I stride seventy-three-point-two miles
to avoid returning to the scene of my earthly disgrace.

I go to the beach. Every day
on the hot sands, chocolate children
with tequila-infused nougaty centers
leave footprints like dogshit smears.
Every day I bring their filthy steps
back to the garden as bribes: "There!
You are fertilized! Shut up!"
And it works for a while, it works until
You Know What opens their craws
and croaks out a litany of vegetable sins.
They'll hear of me on agricultural reports far and wide.
I don't have so much as a soybean future in this town.

Archer Daniels Midland wants to friend me on Facebook.
But I know what it really wants.

THE STORY BEHIND MY NEXT TATTOO

There's a woman parading about
with faces where her holes should be,
swanning about and grinning at every orifice.

She went to the fancy plastic surgeon's office
over on Figueroa, in the medical center
with the deadpan pansies outside,
just to show off and speak Swedish
and Swahili simultaneously.

I call her Mother, though she's a little too young,
but she doesn't object
because she has noses and silver-belled throats and
hazel eyes instead of eardrums, even waxy ones.

She cries, "Look at me! Look and marvel!"
with the mouth in her mouth,
its chin nestled in her lower lip.

I fear her and run to her incessantly
like a kitten after a piece of mint dental floss.

Someone must package her, someone
must give her a TV show, someone
must marry her, that exceptional kisser,
and make her the happiest woman in the world,
an honest woman, no more lisping, distorted lies
from the wee swallow tongues in her orbital sockets.

Will she warble to me in sweet ten-part harmonies when I
      am old?

AVOIDANCE

Let's make believe we're elsewhere.
Let's keep an even keel in the waters of our mind —
a smooth gliding in a taut canvas canoe
on a lake of placid equanimity —
not caught in the crosshairs of status and mishap,
an escape artist locked in an opulent corner office
after swallowing the key.
Let's not listen to Ram Dass. Let's not be here now
in the man's office for the anticipated meeting,
the avuncular pomp due to recent circumstances,
the canning of the human pickle.
Let's not discuss the events leading up to this moment:
a divorce, a stubborn repetition of nightcaps,
a morning kicking-in of windows,
a request to deposit one's stink away from
the chaperoned students, first temporarily, then
        permanently.
There and then, there and then, there and then,
the oars dip in from side to side.
Let's make believe cause will not lead to effect,
that we can avoid coming in hard
onto the shore of consequence,
instead spend our days describing lovely circles
out over the depths. Let's just ignore the ripping sound.
Let us never begin.

ACCOUNTING TIME

I have two and a quarter degrees and a dollop of ambition.
I have $5.78 for food, gas, and expenses until next Friday.
Next Wednesday's poetry reading costs three dollars.

Many universities want to take my baby away. It's very
important to improve ourselves through higher education.

We have almost two packages of generic hot dogs,
three small Baggies of frozen fish fillets, and a half-eaten,
uncovered pork chop, still antless, from four days ago.

I have work over there and over there. She has work down
        there.
She takes classes for a better life. I teach classes to students
with classic cars, horses, bus passes, and skateboards.

We have full tanks of gas. We could go almost anywhere,
either of us. We've been planning a day trip since February.

My wife has made me happy. Six years and counting.
We count the days, gauging each one by the night's
television programming. Monday nights are the best.

We have about a dozen cans of food, mostly black olives.
I like olives much more than she. They don't make a meal.

I have 140 freshman-composition essays to grade over these
two weeks. I have one week left. Poetry stands in my way.
Poetry makes me happy except for when it doesn't.
Poetry and grocery bills live in two different worlds.

I still have some money in my retirement accounts, unfed
since 2007. The IRS is still hungry for most of its money
from when we liquidated a third of the holdings in 2008.

She woke up upset because I hadn't cooked anything,
          because
there was no food waiting for her. What was she expecting?

We have two partial bags of granola, seven economy packs
of sugarless gum, a bag of potatoes, and a bag of onions.

I sit in my car Monday mornings, afraid to go to work.
What if they smell what a disappointment I've become?
A slice of pizza might fill the hole in my wallet-sized soul.

I haven't paid a credit-card bill since July. Why bother?
The cards have been over the limits and useless since June.

When she came to me from Manila, her family was left
without its breadwinner. She thought she was coming
to a better one in a better position. I had a different job then.
Then I had another different job. Now I have these three.

We have half a loaf of bread, its slices like buns for the hot
          dogs.
We have lots of pickle relish. Does it taste good over rice?

Looking at all of the challenges and opportunities our life
amply provides, today is the day I take charge of this poem.
Today is when everything changes, within these lines.

RESPITE

At two in the afternoon, it often seems
the man in the apartment next to me
pours into his thermos a quart of cocktails
looking and smelling like vodka and tonic
(not always my favorite) gets into his trunks,
blows up his inflatable lounge chair, and
goes to the pool, floating, slowly drinking for hours.

At two in the afternoon, I sit on my balcony
and sip bottles of King Cobra malt liquor
out of a clean glass, like a professional,
classy gentleman of leisure. I lean back
and watch hummingbirds pivot and swoop
around the branches of the closest tree,
looking for something among the blossomless leaves.
Whatever they find, I sincerely hope that
they don't let the smooth taste fool them.

I recall the Persian chicken joint down the road
from my old job, back when I worked full-time
among friends, where I would take a late lunch
at two in the afternoon, where the people made
a dish combining delicious rice with green beans
and the slightest hint of something wonderful
to remind its customers of lost homes or distant lands.

This place had no liquor license, so I used to order
salty, minted, thin yogurt over ice. If
it were only safe to drive right now, if
I had money to spare from the drinking fund,
I might lasso a hummingbird and return
to the restaurant, flying over the pool
to call to my neighbor, asking if I could
pick him up anything, anything at all.

SHORT STACK

On South Ashley Street
we position ourselves

in a trailer cathedral of sunrise,
a venerable hipster holding pen.

in an Ann Arbor canon,
in a menu fingerprinted with syrup,

in flannel and blue jeans,
we slouch in the booth, light up,

drink coffee and order,
ignoring the hippie hash

and the earnestness of vegan entrees.
What later anoints our foreheads—

December perpetually
frothy with cold temple blood—

as we wipe away Brady's unspoken
departure and stray locks of hair,

are smears of butter whipped
for pancakes in the diner kitchen

and the ashes from cigarettes
flicked onto empty plates.

DRIVING BACK TO THE HALFWAY HOUSE

SLKMNS: Silk Moans (a stylish Goth band)?
Solo kimonos (Han's Orientalist transvestitism)?
Nobody knows what the license plate means,
the source of the vanity in the car ahead.

When younger-Eric-my-friend, in the center
of the second row of backseats, opines that
his favorite guess so far is "Slowly loving to kill

motherfucking Depeche Mode," everyone else
hoots so loud that I worry they'll wake up
and rile the supervisor dozing next to me.

No real good will come of that at all. Even if
the clients are all hoots, they are all hoots
for the wrong reasons, hoots like I used to be,
before they straightened out my primary meds.

Anything you decide, Maria, ever hootless,
must be so! We exhale easily only when
you are not cranky. Your breath always
unduly sways our air. Our conversations

are brief and eclipsed by the shadow of your pen,
writing reports and assigning demerits. And yet...
People evolve and move away over time
like splayfoot hominids crossing the savannah;

But you stay in the trees, these Shady Maples,
wielding simple tools like me, a half-splintered
limb in a rude vine apparatus, a crooked branch
slowly sharpened by irregular abrasiveness.

Once, before I learned to drink, back before I learned to drive, I used to read books in the car, not yet truly understanding what *slack* means.

KING OF THE ROAD

On or about, I ambled as best I could, aware
they watched through the windows,
past the trees I had carved from spite,

up the long, straight path, one foot
at a time on the asphalt, one foot
at a time in the air, testing the breeze.

Where all the signposts bear my name
is a hideous form of neighborhood.

Over my shoulder hung a bindle
of silk and mahogany, soft and opulent.

The leaves fell like playing cards, wormholes
like pips, and lay clustered on the green ground
like gin rummy hands at a hobo camp.

I scanned the stray cat and the boxcar,
the robin and the iron yoke of tracks,
each with a separate destination
hidden within the folds of the hills.

The robin spoke with my voice,
called out for a day's work and caviar:
chopping wood, mending fences,
green-black oil from plump Beluga roe.

The wind carried the bird away.
My résumé ceased to develop
until my *coup d'etat* could resume.

LOST SCENT, STRANGE MOUNTAINS

My first marriage and kidneys failed
surrounded by San Jose pho shops
emitting a fragrance I love. It took
nine years of passive aggression
before she flew to New Zealand
and I drove to Reno with a scabby cat,
early 2003, an excellent season for
star anise, strips of flank steak, and idle
reflections on blood in the urine.
We contemplate insurance fraud,
my cat and I, neither of us any longer
covered by her comprehensive policy,
which would even have handled the vet.
I put him to sleep myself, crusty fur,
fish breath, and all, as promised.

Trip-hop mills the burrs from nerves
oversharpened by bottomless casino
coffee cups. Over the bass undertow
of dZihan & Kamien, I text my doctor,
the perky nephrologist, to schedule
more dialysis, more slow hours during
which to consider divorce as an iPod
left out in the rain, draining all future
batteries despite their insertion with care.
Nothing is Vietnamese in this new town.
Nineveh, Machiavellian, wicked but
lacking Babylon's cool, the herbs of Saigon.
I sit like a damp, spastic machine, casing
cracked. One napkin, two napkins, three
napkins only begin to mop up the mess.

KEEP THE HOME FIRES BURNING

Pale parking-lot moon, a sliver
of stray toenail I want to bite off and chew.

Just beneath, the sign says Motel 6
charges a bundle these days:
not worth the injury when
the meth lab the next unit over goes boom.

Dark shells of cars cause me to recollect likely
tweakers slimjimming my Honda in spring
around three AM,
grabbing the black backseat bag,
nothing inside of worth, nothing
outside paper stacks, stray moon
rocks, stomach lint.

I would have limped after them
had I known as it occurred.
How could they touch me?
Didn't anyone see?

Sparks of light, satellites
pass me by overhead, screening
and discounting larcenies for
the sake of national security, for
perception instead of reality.

My molars grind like lapdancers
making the rent on a Monday.

Break out the keycard; time to go in.
Time to go sleep in fresh sheets.
Nothing at night is the best reward.

EATING OUT

Like a moth to the grease fire, I head inside
to the counter to look at the menu, at thick
oiled sandwiches and half-chickens, skin

almost crisp where it's blackened, the result
of charring and steam tables, at combo meals.
I try to catch the cashier's eye, but she spits

out her spiel while staring away at wall tiles,
looking down now and again to press buttons
with pictures on the semiautomatic register.

Here, at this place, the mavens of eating locally,
of regional cuisine, must arrive, touch their lips,
and head to their cars to MapQuest a bistro,

as I should, looking around at this place, a place
like the place near my home, far away, also filled
with fluorescent lights, French fries, and strangers.

HOMETOWN EXPATRIATE

Returning from twenty years of renters' purgatory
on the West Coast, looking for permits at city hall,
I was sent into a bout of bureaucratic bumper cars
by the daughter of my mother's ex-best friend, who
may have remembered me, may have meant the best
for me, or one of two. A breeze off the lake brought
the burnt-sock smell of early-morning brimstone left
from firing shotguns into the air to scare flocks of
incontinent geese away from the waterfront park.

I read the local newspaper's awful features section
and already missed ethnic restaurants. They don't
make sushi from bluegills and red-eared sunfish.
I was surprised to be kicked off the beach for lacking
proper tags by a lifeguard alive fewer years than
I had lived here. I pointed up the hill to the spot
where my childhood house stood before it was razed
for a flashy McMansion. There was a story in that,
and chronic plantar fasciitis still leaves me feeling like
a perceptive Fisher King, but limping along slowly
in flip-flops, I arrived too late to hear of the scandal.

At the local bar, they offered me lake water to drink,
a joke, a huge glass jug of green liquid almost as large
and transparent as my delusion of being a prophet
returned to his homeland, ready to make changes
to how daily bread was ground into ethical crumbs.

I had been among the first children to try escargot
back when the market began stocking tins of them,
so I had wrongly assumed a sort of advantage.

Later, walking past the address where my home had been, I saw an old classmate through the bay window, and she who had once freely chased and been chased for kisses around primary-school playgrounds now lounged in dim light with a glass of something dry and maroon they didn't drink in the old days. Off I crept, sweeping myself down the street, tumbling backwards, caught in a circle of my own choosing.

AN AREA BOUNDED BY THREE SURFACE STREETS

Our neighborhood blossoms lutescent with dry-aged
sides of sunburn on slow-walking grandmothers and

immature dandelions. Frozen cubes of ground basil
lose their flavor in every home freezer. It has one pair

of new Wal-Mart sneakers thrown over a power line
outside the apartment complex, size nine, I'd guess.

It acts as a magnet for uncle-touching Santa Ana winds
that blow colder and colder each year. Our neighborhood

was meticulously designed by a master planner long
after the syphilis kicked in. Its streets arc like chip shots

intended as penalty kicks, high hidden slopes that test
brakes and cause accidents with native squirrels. But

it has no knowledge of meanness, only the rules of real-
world McDonalds Monopoly. It seems to speak to us

sometimes: We need ice-cream socials and taco-eating
contests to solder your lips in solidarity, hidden mikes

near the traffic cameras to record the tenor whalesongs
of your passes through me. It floats on a grimy tectonic

hubcap balanced on the back of an underground turtle,
spinning us gently along through history and space.

ISLAND LIVING

San Francostco covers the entire peninsula,
geographical thumbnail to wrist, offering
fifty-seven thousand kinds of free samples of

laminated manna no doctors allow themselves
to eat. This is a soulful, mind-blowing
theme park beyond all mortal ken, encircling

concept, life, and death; expired shoppers
culminate in the south of the store. You can
pick up fifty gallons of cioppino in a crusty

sourdough bucket; you can purchase a barrel
of tomato-and-garlic-flavored chum. You can
buy bushels of hydroponic arugula harvested

fresh from the ceiling that morning, right near
the top of the structure, in Mariners Marketers
Managers Heights. On the lower floors, mobs

of shoppers are entertained by the lion dancers,
coupons scattering like paper beard-dandruff
from their shaken manes, and by the sudden

formations of critical masses of synchronized
forklifts, blocking pedestrian traffic for only
the most ideologically sound of reasons:

the economy must be stimulated. But you tire,
you miss your car. Your children have stealthily
wandered off to find the talking salmon. You

must go. Did you park far to the east, in the
vast asphalt prairies of Contra Costa County?
Did you ride the Bay Escalator to arrive? You

don't remember, you don't think so. So look
past the towering grill shaped like firemen
rampant in coitus. Look past the milling

crowds of militant boy-whores, tender-loined
crack commandos wearing beef bouffants.
Make your way down the aisles through the

piles of rainbow gymwear, past the inflatable
burrito mission, past the unctuous racks of
fried town hangers, through the valleys and

over twin peaks. Pass under the ceremonial
golden gateway entirely surrounded by
clicking tourists and sniff your way down the

scent trail of patchouli, crab dungeons, and
espresso. Every few hundred steps, an
employee who hates you asks for change, a toll

paid for living without tattoos or tongue-rings.
Go through the doors marked "THEM ONLY,"
between the fog machines, into the sunset. Go

there, tangent to the inscrutable Pacific Rim,
the next store over. Listen for the seagulls and
surf machines, scrawing above and washing

your clothes, shitting and rinsing, eating the
leftover hotdog a chunky boy bought at the
concession on Level 86P, laving the dirt from

the denim, the mustard from the muslin. Take
a deep breath and relax. There are sharks out
there in the water, waiting for apeseals to close

their eyes. But you are still safe on tile, damp
particles of ground linoleum squishing between
your toes. You are still beneath the fluorescent dome,

breathing the best air that suits your snug budget,
feeling the breeze from the air-conditioning vents.
You have not left. Reach, touch the wall of home.

DOCUMENTED IMMIGRANT

Witness the dormant glory of Romulus Augustus,
arguably the last Western Roman emperor, taking
a nap on an army-surplus cot in the back of the lab.

They had pulled him screaming through the tesseract
almost entirely just before the translucent gyre retracted,
snipping off part of his left big toe, just past the joint.

Some of the research team cleaned and dressed his injury,
white coats, jumbled apologies, bloody water, stitches,
while the rest cheered and gave one another high-fives.

In the context of the community of physical scientists,
trans-temporal engineering would be the new black,
though black itself remains perennially cool, man.

They sent out for meaty pizzas and scholars of antiquity,
hungry to learn whom they had blindly snagged with
their half-imaginary quark-knotting fishing net.

The historically-usurped teenager cried out for Orestes,
Jesus, Jupiter, Fortuna, whichever relative, small god
or saint looks after lost toe pieces, many deaf, dead ears,

and then he wept as regally as he could manage, sobbing
quietly, snot majestically trickling down his upper lip,
while wincing at the pain. Was pain the ticket to Heaven?

One of the kinder-seeming physicists brought a wheelchair,
helped him hobble into it, still proud, teary and bewildered,
loaded him into the antiseptic hyperbaric chamber for
        testing.

Weeks passed and needles happened. Interviews piled up
around him like sofa cushions stuffed with dictionaries,
a fort of inquisitive words. *Quid? Quis? Ubi? Cur, o cur?*

He explained the best he could the political landscape,
the smell of Odoacer's horsemen and the pity that led to
a life uncurtailed and a post-abdication villa in Campania.

He told them *garum* tasted most like Filipino *patis*, more so
than *nuoc mam* or Chinese fish paste. He liked ice cream,
MMA matches, posters with kittens, and *American Idol*.

He once became enraged and defensive when they laughed
at him for rubbing vanilla Haagen-Dazs on his toe wound –
"Is that Roman folk medicine, 'Roam-oo-leh'?" Bastards!

Fine! You get dragged to twenty-first-century Livermore!
It's confusing! The ice cream helps, all aches subsiding.
They wouldn't give him a concubine, so he had made do.

Months accumulated, and the team that had harvested him
moved on to more lucrative gigs in the private sector. The
        last
once-emperor stayed behind, watching the funding dry up.

Enthroned at fourteen and now, at nineteen or 1,549, last
        year's
science-fair project, still walking and talking funny. No more
royal allowance, worse spaghetti in the cafeteria, strangers.

Watch him fret in his Boy Scout sleeping bag, dreaming
of Italy and cyclotrons, restless, feeling like an unlucky coin
flipped in the air between someone else's finger and thumb.

EXCHANGE RATES

Two hundred miles or more northeast from here
is a mountain that had been sacred
to the proud local indigenous people
for millennia, a mountain named after
the white pioneer who accidentally discovered it,
one crisp cracker of a century ago,
the only name Google Maps and AAA call true.
The mountain had an original name in the language
of the proud local indigenous people,
a name that meant "Little Great Auntie,"
a name that combined age, dignified bearing,
and an affectionate diminutive, a name
I cannot pronounce with the gnarled, slurring tongue
I inherited from my own barbarian forebears.

The first white man to speak without firearms
to the proud local indigenous people
was an anthropologist cross-trained
in linguistics and economics. He taught
the proud local indigenous people
English grammar by repeating,
"*Happiness* was in the apple you gave me.
Happiness *was* the apple you gave me.
Happiness was the *giving* of the apple to me.
Happiness was *in* the giving of the apple to me.
Happiness has a *use* value.
Happiness has an *exchange* value.
Happiness is a *commodity*.
Happiness is a gift." He made
the little proud local indigenous children
happy by giving them apples after their lessons.
In accepting them, the way was paved for
little proud local indigenous children to become
commodities. You can see them today, selling
authentic proud local indigenous pots and rugs,
posing for photographs in Taiwanese polyester replicas
of traditional proud local indigenous garb.

I am not proud, or local, or indigenous.
I am a cowardly European-American mutt
transplanted from a flat spot in the Midwest.
Other white people came many moons ago
to the locales of my formerly proud ancestors,
then still indigenous to certain villages and bogs,
to give them apples, beatings, and English
in exchange for their daughters,
for their whisky, spices, and potatoes.
Now my family simply assumes we come from
Whitelandia, a mythical, chilly, deracinated realm
of bland food and mayonnaise glaciers.
The only ones still speaking the old languages
are fairies on empty cereal boxes and deaf prunes
in nursing homes, commodities with
limited use values, no longer fit for exchange.

POEM FOR CHRISTY'S DAUGHTER

Man Yi is a fading phantom.
Maeve remains solidly planted in the middle of the
      continent.

Maeve knows how to operate chopsticks
only because her roundeye parents taught her
right after she learned to use fork and spoon.

Maybe someday, she'll dye her hair her mother's shade of
      red.
Maybe someday, she'll become a Potato King.

Maeve is not yet trendy.
Maeve is not pan-Asian cuisine.
She does not provide a delightful ginger-and-soy flavor
      profile upon the tongue.

Maeve is not the newest model from Toyota.
Maeve is not Japanese, but *gaijin*.
Maeve is not *gwei lo*.

Maeve does not smell of kimchi, except when she eats
      kimchi.
I do not think Maeve would like kimchi.

Do you remember Manila's humidity and millions?
Maeve does not.

Maeve comes from a place.
Maeve lives in a place.
They are not the same place.
You don't live where you came from, either,
No matter how you struggle to fit inside.

ANYBODY CAN LIVE ON THE MOON

Anybody can live on the moon. Anybody can get
there and set up a homestead, a yurt made of quilted
American and Soviet flags. Up in the sky is a spot
where the rents are not crushing, with Roquefort
rocks free for the chucking or crumbling on salads,

where lost socks commingle with rabbits mixing
liquids of life, immortalizing broths from their own
braised haunches. You fear the alleged airlessness
but overlook the hardly serene selenic atmosphere,
provenance of halos buzzing around the heads of

lunatics, lovers, poets, it's true, but also cheese-
makers, drag-racer pit crews, Monday charcoal
barbecuers, and bus drivers' wives. Think about
the fizzing galas to stage in the craters; maybe some
can be yours! So get in the empty refrigerator box

tucked in the catapult bucket. Hold onto your carry-
on luggage and pull the cord. Something will almost
certainly occur. After the time of utter blackness,
there you'll be, in a new place different and shining,
unbounded from the weight of the waking earth.

HYPOTHESIS

The heathen chefs inform us the salmon of knowledge
tastes better when coated with teriyaki glaze, West
meeting East in the quest for global omniscience. Yet

such culinary lore grows moot as the limitations of large-
scale aquaculture produce many lesser *piscis sapiens*,
each farmed fish specializing in only one of ten thousand

subdisciplines: Irish mythology, Japanese grilling methods,
cheese-curd production, household stain removal, alluvial-
deposit analysis. As the blend of forage fish, bird bits, and

magical hazelnuts chums the water in the pens, creating
a reddish-gray cloud of debatable nutrition and potency,
many alevin swim about, consuming the flecks. If the only

criteria for wisdom were information architecture and data
retrieval design, these silvery, shadowy flickers that flit
like electrons or sourceless memes around and against

one another, burbling their facts, the narrow prowess of
their proofs and analyses, would emulate a cloud computer,
the next wet generation of hardware leading us all back

to the sea whence we sprang, reclaiming Atlantis with
the help of our finny friends, where all things must leap,
both logically and intuitively arching their backs, their

bodies, our bodies, collectively writing recursively in
the waves, the inscriptions perhaps washed away, perhaps
echoing shore to shore, enmeshed in the currents, patterns

beyond binary, each damp inhabitant spawning focused niblets of knowledge, general schools of thought caught in the tides, avoiding the undertow threatening all experts.

RECIPE FOR A HEX

Call for a sterling-silver
witch's dustpan,
for a bucket of wheat
paste, a black tar
golliwog for snaring sly
rabbits. Call for
pink clutch purses with
toothed apertures,
a whiskered cat skull —
call for patience.

But even with the fetishes
surrounding you,
with the low pulse of mojo
humming beneath
the macramé rug, it will
still be tough to find
enough stray casings to
chew, to spit forth
the immensity of the spell
to reclaim credit.

It's memory that furnishes
debt, filling
the mind's house with
alien tchotchkes and
antique wooden hymnal
stands, with shin-
cracking invisible tables
and dark windows,
all for a price higher than a
sage's wages.

It will take years to write
down on paper
exactly what you know
and what you owe,
an enchanting ledger
intended for absent
descendants, but more
likely to pique the eye
of a historian combing
boxes at the estate sale.

LEGACY

I get a shower stall filled with eleven varieties of
hanging salumi, and a veritable forest of beanstalks,
and the halcyon days of a middle-aged, thundering
wererhino. I get baggies of cumin and coriander for

tikka masala, and roses from the infant's cheeks, and
from the West, premonitions of future events. I get odd,
sultry, slanted insinuations from the vertical blinds, fully
heartsick when the power fails in winter during a heated

cooking competition, and my wife a tidy kilogram of
understanding, sliced and packed in plastic for easy storage
and consumption. I get the stepson reflection of the setting
sun off traffic-baffled rear windows on the 405, and pointless

qualms that prevent me from checking the inbox of my
secondary email account. But I did not get the others in
trouble with destiny despite its arrival amid pallid, fatal
threadsnipping to drag them beneath the skin of the world.

ORGANIC CHEMISTRY

The memory of stepping in gasoline barefoot soaked
        through
my forehead and fired a litany of aches through my chakras.
Ayurvedic principles have tended to contend poorly with
        hydrocarbons.
Ayurvedic principles cannot remove crude from down,
plastic six-pack rings from the tangled necks of cormorants.

With new medical procedures that are not valid medical
        procedures,
we have split the soul into six microwavable servings,
which means two from each family of four can have seconds.
Nobody calls us to dinner.
Walk perpendicular to the kitchen table, widdershins
around the deacon's bench next to the door painted shut.
Our appetite for oily sauces speaks louder than words.

There are moments when missing certain species is rote
        silence during roll call.
This is not one of them. There are moments when missing
        certain species
is soft like nostalgia, a falling of acid snow or ash,
when only small ceramic replicas of Eastern Cougars or
        honeybees
can choke the pain in its bassinet. Let us offer Twinkies and
        nylon money
to the household gods and pray for petrochemical fires.
Benzene, Benzedrine, toluene, charred tollbooth residues: we
        are
the offspring of volatile essences, driving to Valhalla on
        vapors.

ECO-POEM

Back before nature was handed
over to the ants and the manufacturers,
when it sat outside your kitchen window
and sang you songs of mystery and cyclicity,
when snails crept from the ground up your legs
up your body to your face
to leave tracks across your cheeks
and embed love-darts in your lips,
when the pieces they called "grass"
spread across the unpavement,
when what they called "trees,"
those stick-things, swayed in a wind
that was not yet like a blow-dryer,
I bore nature no mind.
I did not care about the fine gray soil.
I did not care about the smooth gray sea.
I did not care about the bright gray sky.
Now I bring the children to vending machines
to buy discrete units of nature:
bottles of clean water,
canisters of fresh air,
rectangular packages labeled
"Protein-Flavored" and "Drywall & Corn Syrup,"
bags of recycled soy jerky.
It's only natural to feel some regret.

RECONQUISTA

A late-night fast-food restaurant employee
nods off at his station, sitting on a milk crate,
trying to lean without touching the wall.
As he fades, the Mega Bean-n-Cheezer Burrito
sprouts fanged cockatrice head, coiled tail
scaled with foil wrappers, wings feathered
with skateboard decks, flies over the microwaves,
a faux-Mexican faux-edible Quetzalcoatl on
a mission of vengeance. It doesn't want
the return of Aztlan. It doesn't want
a renegotiated Treaty of Guadalupe Hidalgo.
It doesn't want a warm beating heart
from the near-virgin at the drive-thru.
It just wants less wood pulp in the ground "meat,"
more dairy in the "cheez topping," It shrieks
"not a bang but a whimper" in Nahuatl
as it flutters, soars, dives through the door
of the manager's office for the redress,
for the rending, for razor claws unzipping a neck
like a packet of Mucho Fuego hot sauce.
Here comes the culinary Reconquista.
Here comes the time of obsidian chef's knives,
honest butchery of cows and industrial chemists,
Xipe Totec returned in a toque clipped from their skins.
Here come the drums and the banners, the rumble
of drums like the sound of the fans in the hoods,
the fans in the hoods, the gurgle of grease in the fryers.
The timer goes off when the fries are done,
awakening the napping boy, reeling but alert
to the red and gold world of tomorrow.

ODE TO BARABBAS

Barabbas, Barabbas, you bad Jew, Barabbas. A coin to
the temple, some bread for your grandma and alms in
the dust at the feet of the beggars of Yahweh do not make
you righteous, Barabbas. Barabbas, so burly, Barabbas,

so noisy, your greasy black chin-curls abob as you're stirring
up masses of louts playing patriots, churning Masadan
bravado for fortresses made out of boozy breath, guarded by
hooligans snug in their dreams in the neighborhood taverns.

A big-city mugger, Barabbas jacks tourists at swordpoint,
exchanging their safety for shekels he squanders on botas
and booty, on shitty wine, lousy quim, one of them maybe
your cousin, Barabbas, or doesn't that matter when juices

are running high? Somebody saw her one avenue over
the other day, asking about you, but you will not visit,
Barabbas, not now that your appetite's faded. Just why did
they save you, Barabbas, and why did they call out your
      name

for release on Golgotha? The storekeepers sprinkled
throughout the crowd wanted you living to pay off your
debts to them, groceries purchased on credit, amphorae
of oil and liquor, kebab meat, and pitas. Your buddies

felt loyal, beholden; your eyes caught their faces and raised
a brow. Aunties in black linen dresses remembered your
boyhood and softened. The Greek-loving cynics preferred
      you
to that one, the Nazarene, carpenter-fisherman-maniac

pattering earnestness, lamb's wool and guilt-tripping
salesmanship. Some of the sillier teenagers found you
a Byronic hero, a Jesse-James outlaw, Barabbas the Ballsy.
But most of the people just wanted to piss off the Romans,

who hated your swaggering bullshit, which echoed too
closely their own. And they freed you, Barabbas, they took
you down, faking some grins for the audience. "Here's your
guy, everything's cool," and they yanked you down,

tossed you your tunic, and led you offstage into darkness,
where legionnaires grabbed your arms, holding you tight
while the legion commander let punches fly. Two of your
molars flew onto the concrete and tumbled like dice

to the feet of the soldiers, who hooted and finally booted
you into the alley, to liberty, muttering vengeance but
having the animal sense to get up and get going, away
to your house for some respite and possibly, bandages.

Jesus bar-Abbas, the son of the father, godfather of pogroms,
they'll blame your alleged Semitic parole board, those
blonde-bearded rednecks igniting your so-many-great-
nephews' silos and cottages, cross-eyed with fury and

intimate envy. For now, are you up to your old tricks,
Barabbas, out prowling Jerusalem, coldcocking
          nightwalkers,
taking their wallets, then blatantly stealing the waitresses'
tips off the tables, aware that they can't do a thing to you,

boasting of how you get by? Do you ever reflect on your
fortune and trickle some drink on the ground, saying,
"Sorry, bro, better you, better than I"? What or whom do
          you
wrestle, Barabbas, what or who will attend when you die?

STOREFRONT CHURCH

They got slammed over at St. Mel's this weekend, the short-order priest in his Roman collar and apron dealing with six orders up, anointing with consecrated butter the ovoid foreheads of a half-dozen separate infants and fully immersing them in the warm, wet insides of the unplugged ice machine. And after each dunking, after the clapping had subsided, it was time for a homily and for slipping charred disks of cut-up hot dogs onto the tongues of the communicants filling the booths and lining the aisles. For the special was "Buy one baptism, get a free Mass." With six on his plate, he didn't have a chance to sweep the nave, scrape the grill or count the receipts until closing time.

This was the busiest time since old Monsignor Nick accidentally blessed a case of 7-Up, transubstantiating it into the lymph of Christ. Once word got out, every thirsty Catholic with a spiritual infection had stormed the glass doors, hoping to procure some of the limited supply and sluice away the pus from the cankers in their soul. One man, who hadn't spoken with his sister for years due to some forgotten offense, had called her on the pay phone outside and planned a family meal. That heartening story made it into the bulletin the following week.

Let the Episcopalians have their *bifteck au poivre avec pommes frites*. Leave the kashi and wheatgrass for the Unitarians. This is the center of a working-class parish, favoring honest, hearty, American food: burgers, pepper steak and fries, corned beef and cabbage on Tuesdays, spaghetti with meatballs on Wednesdays, golabki on Thursdays, fish and chips on Fridays. Look for the neon crucifix above the front door. If you're in a rush, use the drive-thru, filled with carloads of cowlicked teenagers in their best T-shirts and limousines of young grooms screwing curly fries onto the ring fingers of their new wives. Come empty, leave full.

LEFT BEHIND

Who doesn't remember [THIS] sound, a tone
so loud it wrapped around and became
perfect sublime stillness again,
a sound that left my earplugs bloody?
Who doesn't remember the noontime aurora borealis?
The empty cars littering the 405?

Yes, oh yes. Everyone realizes but
nobody mentions how much we miss
the days before May 21, 2011,
the world before the Rapture.

Everyone misses the long, mahogany stables
of neon-colored pegasi, who flew
because of the ethereal perfection of their souls,
who flew right out of sight that fateful day,
bearing away all Scorpio meteorologists.
True, men couldn't have sex with these beautiful pegasi
because of the invisible, carnivorous chickens
living symbiotically inside their bowels and vaginas,
but they were still nice to masturbate to.

And where is the Pop-Tart lottery of yesteryear?
Millions invested their breakfasts with hope and
anticipation,
breaking the Pop-Tarts open like fortune cookies,
hoping for a winning ticket that would allow
them to marry an extra spouse,
just in case of emergencies,
like if the original spouse fell into a cistern or a septic tank.
When I won, I married a goat,
partly to annoy Raquel,
partly in a misguided attempt to please and impress
a South-African-American freelance web designer.
He's gone now, too.
Dengue fever.

My husband didn't mind the goat, but he was cool like that.
He was one of the ninety-nine percent of homosexuals
that ascended directly into Heaven that day.
Who would guess, looking around lately,
that they used to outnumber straight people by such a wide
margin?

Now we abandoned individuals wander aimlessly,
intermittently watching reality television,
getting fattening snacks from the pantry,
channel-surfing at Mach speeds,
waiting for one of us to sprout horns
so we can cry, "Hail, wicked leader!
Lead us into the fiery abyss!
There's nothing good on anymore, nothing good at all."

PILGRIM'S PROGRESS

If you squeeze the sleaziness from your heart
as if you are making fresh mozzarella or tofu,
you may end up with a chest of pristine curds,
and when you move on from this world,
you may tell the cosmic chefs that parts of you

befit even the finest Caprese salads and stir-fries.
A giant oven will stand preheated, ready to engage
with your exercises in self-basting and rotisserie
genuflection. It is hot, make no mistake, but not hellishly,
more purgatorially so, more inclined to grant you

the golden, glistening skin you've always deserved,
at least ever since you stopped slapping strangers' kids
when they wouldn't stop screaming at Albertson's,
ever since you quit spending rent money on whiskey
and then lying to your wife as you lay in bed late at night.

To rephrase, you will become the most excellent foodstuffs
eventually, now that you have been harvested from
the earthly garden, plucked from the terrestrial barnyard,
and nobody can stop you from achieving your true karmic
destiny of laying on God's dinner plate, hopeful, delicious.

OTHER ANAPHORA LITERARY PRESS TITLES

Michael Connelly
By Stan Schatt

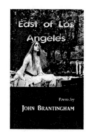

East of Los Angeles
By John Brantingham

Death Is Not the Worst Thing
By T. Anders Carson

Folk Concert
By Janet Ruth Heller

100 Years of the Federal Reserve
By Marie Bussing-Burks

River Bends in Time
By Glen A. Mazis

Interviews with BFF Winners
By Anna Faktorovich, Ph.D.

Compartments
By Carol Smallwood

CPSIA information can be obtained at www.ICGtesting.com
Printed in the USA
BVOW011800070113

310006BV00001B/91/P